Window over the Sink

Prose Poems

by

Charles Springer

Fernwood
PRESS

Window over the Sink

Fernwood Press
Newberg, Oregon
www.fernwoodpress.com

Printed in the United States of America

Cover and page design: Mareesa Fawver Moss
Cover photo: Vincent Camacho
Author photo: Maura Koeller

ISBN 978-1-59498-141-8

Frank Norris famously said that he could not stand "the Tragedy of the Broken Teacup," referring to the regular domestic realism of his day. Today, in the prodigious and prodigal irreal prose of *Window over the Sink*, Charles Springer smashes the good china to bits, and, at the same time, *kintsugis* the shards back together with a precious breathless syntactically gorgeous grout. He gives us tragedy, sure, but also the whole Polonius litany of "tragical-comical-historical-pastoral-poem unlimited" in this very real surreality. *Window over the Sink* is the whole kitchen reno—a pantry of the beatific and bestial, a cabinet of wonderful wonders. Springer's panache puts a Good Housekeeping Seal of Approval on the whole crazy spread of this out-of-control mad tea party of a book.

—Michael Martone

author of *Plain Air: Sketches from Winesburg, Indiana* and *The Complete Writings of Art Smith, The Bird Boy of Fort Wayne,* edited by *Michael Martone.*

In the tradition of James Tate and Russell Edson, Charley Springer creates prose poems that sing with absurdity. Sometimes his opening lines start off innocently, with no warning of the zany world you are about to enter. More often, however, he gives you a clue that just ahead lies the Springer world, where reality is optional. No matter where Springer takes you, it's bound to lead to an intriguing place, with likable characters and an ending you did not anticipate. His literary high jinks and verbal gymnastics on the page are a joy to watch. My favorite poem in the collection is "Wilds," which opens with a sighting of wild turkeys, followed by a progression of wild hogs, wild one-eyed Jacks, wild hair, a wild goose, and culminating in the songs "Born to be Wild" and "Wild Things, I Think I Love You." The end result is a mind-boggling work of art and a testament to the poet's skill. A delightful entertaining read that takes poetry to the outer limits of what is possible and shows what a prose poem can do in the right hands.

—Gene Twaronite

Author of four poetry collections,
including *The Museum of Unwearable Shoes* and *Shopping Cart Dreams*

Charles Springer's book of prose poems, *Window over the Sink*, is a tinderbox waiting to set fire to your eyelashes, the hair on the back of your neck, and everything in between. The shapes of these prose poems are accurate: four semi-equal sides holding. Lightly compressing. Pick up the top corner with your eyes, and everything you never thought flies out and settles on your shoulders like tiny sparks sizzling away at preconceived notions, dazzling your pupils with infinite pyrotechnics, and burning your tongue with a whole new language. *Window over the Sink* is the ember inside the itch of a universal burn. Hold this book and feel yourself shoved to the edge of tomorrow.

—Rebecca Kinzie-Bastian
Author of *Charms for Finding*

To those looking out, or in,
who can see past their own reflections.

Contents

One

Can you tell
just by looking at him
he's seen most things?

Door

Anymore Daryl rarely goes anywhere without his door. Most of us are of the opinion it's not his front door as we've seen his front door and his front door's heavy and dark. My wife guesses it's his bathroom door, something for him to get behind when he's out in public and he's got to pee. Sometimes we see Daryl carrying his door by its knobs a little off to his side and if you watch him for any length of time and distance, you'll catch him switching sides with it. Sometimes the wind will catch it and spin him and his door around in a circle or two but he never lets go. We've seen him fall to the ground with the door ending up on top of him, once with him on top of the door but he always gets up and brushes the door off before himself. That speaks volumes about the kind of man Daryl is. Not long ago I saw Daryl, well, me and my wife saw Daryl digging a shallow little trench for it along the riverbank so we stopped and watched. Eventually Daryl set the door upright in this little trench, stepped back and knocked. The door didn't move but everything else did! The entire landscape around us seemed to revolve! My wife and I were flabbergasted but Daryl was unmoved. Just then he turned and invited us in. It was everything you could imagine.

Rooming

I run into this empty room at an open house. The room is looking for a new house but every one it comes to is full. The first house says, try another house. Another house says, not next to my new den you don't. Still another insists the room bring its own purpose. So the room is back on the street. Neighbors look in the room's window. One of them opens it because she never lit up a room before. Last Tuesday a professional paid a house call to listen to the room's roominess. A locksmith undid its deadbolt. Meanwhile the room risks its foundation from setting on too damp ground. And its north wall weakens from wind. Thanks to a thief, an abandoned van finds itself in the room's shadow. If only I had axles and could sprout tires, thinks the room, I would not need a house. I could be my own house wherever I want. I might even roll myself into the path of a tornado and discover some prairieless states, rely on the eye of a hurricane to see me home. Just then, a knock on the room's door from a lady in a yellow jacket whose every other word sounds like location. I found you the house, the room is able to make out, but you'll have to attach as its porch. I'll be a garage first, the room insists, maybe the owners will fill me with treasures, you know, the ones they tell the rest of the house there is no room for.

Backstage at a Staging

The sign is planted near boxwood hedges in front of the house. They brush against the big bay window where inside a cat and a parakeet play catastrophic footsie on the sill. Keet's just about had enough and jumps to the cat's head and screeches in its ear. Cat's off to the dog for a little backup, meanwhile keet rockets to the pantry and poops in the food dish by the door that leads to the cellar. Was it the cat's or the dog's? The mouse of the house is taking its morning spritz in a puddle whose source is unknown. The owners left early through a back door as the front door is and always will be for show.

Big Leaves

I was talking to my neighbor Henry over the hedge and as he was clipping along, some of its big leaves attached themselves to my cap and coat and some stuck to my corduroys as we moved along the edge and by its end I noticed I'd taken on the topiary version of myself, quite a handsome cut of figure Henry's wife, Lola, agreed and warned me to watch out as all the ladies and one curious gentleman on the block would be pulling on and picking off me if I got too close and I got to laughing pretty hard, we all did and soon enough my big leaves began to fall off by themselves and whisk away in the wind, but just so we didn't forget, my ever-the-reminding wife, Alice, pressed a few between wax papers for an album she was going to keep by the bed.

Virtual Pound

All over the neighborhood dogs are hearing high-pitched whistles inaudible to us humans and they're getting up off their dog beds and walking around with their heads down watching their feet, not like they're learning to dance or anything but counting, calculating, they're taking very deliberate steps and no one in any of the houses is paying attention as the dogs move through every room, into closets, down hallways, in and out of every opened door, careful not to stumble or knock things over with their tails, then each one disappearing just like that and sooner or later someone in the household walks by the TV and there on the screen tuned into The Animal Channel is their dog licking it, having already devoured most of the remote.

Extremities

Fred flopped down on the couch. This time he remembered to take off his shoes and when he did, no feet! Maybe they were still in his shoes. He looked. Nope. Maybe they crawled up his calves or hid out in his socks. Maybe they got stuck between the cushions. Maybe the dog grabbed them in a flash and is chasing them around the backyard this very minute. Nope. Nope. Nope. Then up on the ceiling he saw them dancing their toes off, not really, although the toes were hanging on by a thread. Of course his feet would be dancing; they'd just gotten rid of a big ugly body. And the only way they were coming down is if Fred changed his name to Hank and started walking on his hands, dancing on his hands, actually something he'd always wanted to try, not just for fun but in case the day came when he no longer had feet, but learning to hand walk would take awhile, maybe months, maybe ages, so Fred stayed Fred and his feet stayed up on the ceiling all night into many nights until finally one morning he woke up to find that his feet, look at that, were back on, except now they were on the wrong legs which left him walking in circles, figure eights actually like the professional skaters skate until he finally figured out all he had to do was reach down and switch them. It was as easy as putting socks on over shoes, something he'd often thought about trying. Now he would.

Fountain for Youth

After drinking from a garden hose when he was a teenager cutting grass for money, Derrick would drink from nothing else, not a cup, not a glass, not a can, not even a bottle although he did gulp some bong water once and as you might conclude, this hose thing became his trademark and a problem for adults, but for Derrick the hose deal was no big whoop, he simply wore a couple feet of it around his neck like a collar, no, it wasn't a necklace, and if some smartass got lippy, Derrick pretended to have had a tracheotomy and would gurgle through the hose to scare him off, you see he came to love it the same way one took pride in one's inner tube or sections of saxophone, he even slept with it, showered with it, on occasion put a funnel that he wore on his head under his ball cap in an end of it and drank the rain water coming through the leaky roof like it was going out of style and he was the chosen one to bring it back.

Sunday Drive

Sam tells his wife and kids that when next Sunday rolls around, they'll take that drive he's been promising across the scenic Midwest. No feat to be sneezed at since they live in New Jersey. Sam figures Iowa and Nebraska should only take half the morning. The remainder will go by in a flash so be ready with those cameras! Sunday finally rolls around and in between Bird-in-Hand and Paradise, they stop for gas and for Jilly, Sam's wife to grab some pork rinds. Jilly points with a greasy finger at a cornfield in the distance not too far from the pumps. Let's explore, she coaxes so everyone gets out and goes down a row. In less than a minute they're all lost! They keep going but keep coming to dead ends. Every now and then they see other people, at least they think they do, and the occasional dog, once in awhile a cow, a pig or two and chickens, chickens all over the place ignoring the rows, some even perched on the bigger ears, aren't they the roasting ears, nobody knows, when suddenly it starts to get dark and the stars coming out somehow lead Sam's family back to the car to begin heading home to New Jersey where they tell their friends and neighbors over the next several weeks the Midwest was, well, what can we say, amazing.

Night Dress

Cecil wears a hard hat to bed and keeps it on throughout the night. From what his wife, Syl, has told my wife, Jill, it majorly dents his pillow and fluffing up is futile. I've also heard Cecil's dreams are concussive, something to the tune of orchestrated flying debris! I tell Jill none of this makes sense. If it did, we'd all be wearing hard hats to bed and Jill reminds me she already does along with asbestos panties and steel-toed slippers and a lacy Kevlar teddy and that's when it suddenly occurs to me that for months now, I've been sleeping with some other woman.

Bugs in the Night

A delightful summer evening and Evan is sitting out as close to the middle of his backyard as he can get among the fireflies, they're everywhere, jetting here and jotting there, clustering, a select few forming their own constellation, winking and blinking, nodding in the binoculars, one or two meteoring before Evan's eyes, occasionally one big and bright fly posing as a neighboring planet until one lands on the dog, then others join without invitation waking poor dog up and when Evan goes cross-eyed over the one that just handed on his nose bridge and he meets it eye to eye, he knows it is time to tear up his ticket for the twenty-year-long flight to Polaris, instead become dust right here in his own backyard, having always felt like an old star himself.

Of Youth

I ask Jesse where he met her, this new girlfriend of his, and he says, at the wall, I mean well, and I say, you mean at the bar on the corner and he jumps in with no, no, the well in the center of town where everyone draws water and I come back with, you mean the old fountain in the park, and Jesse says to me in an exasperated sort of way, call it what you will, we drank water, a whole bucket-on-a-rope of it and it was better than carnival sex on a first date, it was nirvana, Jackie and I nearly died on that date, and then's when I jump in with so are you seeing her again, and he says, seeing who, what are you talking about James, I think you need to get out more, get down, get hydrated you ole landlubber you, you old prune.

Commercials

Jay calls to tell me commercials are running in his sleep, they even interrupt his dreams. They never wake me up, he says, but they're there and more vivid than any OBEs. Some run as narrations, some, conversations and many with trumpet accompaniment. They always want money, either as cause-worthy donation or as payment for ordered goods and/or services. I first of all tell Jay how expounding he sounds and that I experienced the very same weeks ago. But they've remained in my room, Jay goes on, they plaster my walls, project on the ceiling so I give him the name of the best commercial exorcist, the one with the cross that doubles as a remote and I tell Jay if this guy's not able to send them on their way, do what I did. Audition. Get in one. It may lead to a role in a soap. Above all, big smile. Bigger. Your biggest!

Elude

Big Earl knows he's missing out when Little Duke hears something he does not, cannot, and when Big Earl asks him, Little Duke's too busy listening to whatever it is that eludes Big Earl. That must be it then, concludes Big Earl, not a prelude, not a postlude, not even a Quaalude but an elude that plays on in Little Duke's furry little ears for minutes at a time, has him repeatedly tilting his head from side to side like he's trying to get water out and it nudges him to whine along to its tune he's tuned into. Now Little Duke's on his feet. He's going in circles. He has no tail to speak of to chase and eventually he just flops down in a nice little heap, head on his rump, eyes mostly closed, breathing as if his life didn't depend on it, as if listening is all he ever had to do.

The Aluminum

It took no genius, only our little Eugene to discover for himself, for us all, the connection between the inventor of the TV dinner and the TV dinner inventor's second cousin, maker of our little cookie cutter plus hundreds, maybe millions out there just like it. Little Eugene had merely plied his fork handle to make some little doorways through the shallow walls of his aluminum tray to let the gravy from the mashed potatoes flood his whole kernel corn and the juice from the cranberry sauce soak his little cornbread square and there we had it as he succinctly stated: physical proof of plot, foreign and/or domestic, alien and/or earthly to homogenize the post-war modern world all in the name of and for the sake of profitable convenience and convenient profit. Hmm, no one in the family could figure how these very words made their way out of our little Eugene's mouth. Personally I think it had something to do with the aluminum.

Dressing

Dexter has only seen the world through a window, he has just the one so when time came for him to go out into the world, he took his window with him, held it out in front of him as he walked and he'd developed the most extraordinary triceps the ladies couldn't take their eyes off and the window itself was what you might call a modified bay to maximize his peripheral viewing and quite unexpectedly nobody bothered Dexter, not one thug threw a rock, not one kid kicked a ball but every now and then someone would indeed walk right up to him and order a burger to go, until one day Dexter asked a passerby to hold the window for him while he bent down to pick something up and when he stood up to take the window back, curtains.

Marks

A young geologist has named the stones that snail across Death Valley's flats when no one watches. Trails they leave behind seem sane unlike the one I roll my eyes about, the swath a bear haphazards through my yard at half past two broadcasting millet, black oil seed from sunflowers, flecks of poplar wood and polypropylene from pawed and smithereened bird feeders. No one but the surgeon and his team can see themselves go in an abdomen. Yet pride after recovery pulls up its shirt. It's no extravaganza run off-Broadway but a drama nonetheless with rounds of dull applause. This poem, its mention here after the phrase about the dull applause is only wandering, a doodle trail like its beginning through revisions, reams of paper products reaching from the can, a ganglia of roots to boost a plum. As is the meteor that tacks on "-ite" inside our atmosphere. I don't care about its ferric content, just my wish I fashion from its tail. Each way I'm moved sardined in subway cars, in trains that whoosh me over tracks and when the whistles blow, I'm less by traces that I've left behind to sewer waters, what with liver, lungs, and kidneys working right up to the clock. My ripe facade will shed its fresco (bow to friction) during sex then rest on sheets and upright as I'm running late to work. Little wonder much remains but who or what's the much, the mover of hot stones, the ursine shaker, scalpel steadier of saving cuts? Who's there, who dictates words to me, stenographer, mad gopher bent on rabbiting the stacks, man of the yard who sifts debris, ooher near a scar, wower at some sparks? Response is sweet and quick, no slight of hand and strictly in my language when I'll truly need to hear.

The One and Only

You know how when you reach for the one on your nightstand, you end up pushing it just out of reach so you have to get up out of bed before you fall out onto the floor and you may as well have fallen out because what you want now is on the floor and when you move toward it, you kick it under the bed and now you have to get down on your hands and knees and lower your head to where you see it is, extend your arm twisting your neck and shoulder and now you are only inches away but inches are inches and may as well be feet so you extend your reach with the yardstick you keep in the corner of the closet and push it farther away into a crack in the hardwood floor, it slipped in perfectly like here is where it came from and for all you know it did and now you'll have to move the bed but where, it practically fills the room and so you look elsewhere, everywhere in the house and after nearly an hour of looking, you discover this was the only one, the one you can't even write your story with now you've got one.

Justice for the Taking

Best night to rob the neighbors is when they're out to dinner and a movie after and you already know pretty much what's inside their house and where it's at but you forgot to bring along some bags and spend half an hour looking for theirs so maybe it's not really burglary when you use the victims' bags, more like borrowing as when your wife asked for a cake plate or the umpteenth plastic storage bowl with burpable lip, if only it could talk, so all you end up taking are some leftovers from their fridge they'd have given you anyway just for the asking and sixteen quarters from a cup on the window sill above the sink, the cup you've been looking for ever since the neighbor's wife's first cup of coffee at your house she supposedly accidentally took with her.

Empties

Eddie's into empties. Glass ones. Green ones. He likes to look through them, says they make his day. A man in a desert built his house out of empties and cement. He gets to look through his walls and keeps dogs who get to look through walls too. Eddie sometimes shoots them, empties that is, off the picket. He's proudest of the ricochet embedded in his forehead. No one has one like it and he won't let the doc take it out though the doc said he'd do it for free. You see, when Eddie gets a little anxious, like when the recycle truck comes, he just reaches up there and pushes it. He calms down some. It makes everyone's day.

Force of Habit

As soon as Buster gets in the door, he kicks his shoes off. It doesn't end there. He kicks them clean across the room, from room to room, even down the stairs into the cellar. It's hard to keep up as there are really four of them when you add in his big leather work mitts he once wore on his feet in a pinch. Dog runs after them like they're puppies, never knows which to go after first and if Buster's in the mood, he keeps right on kicking until they've formed a pack inside the house but this one time, I recall it being a Friday, yes, a Friday, the kicking ended up in the street and Dog was right there in the traffic, mitts on his front paws, shoes on his backs, in a stand-up position, license tag on his choker flashing like a sheriff's badge and surprisingly a number of arrests were made: running a red light, driving without a license, failing to yield to pedestrians with pets and these were all other dogs driving while sitting on their owners' laps, oh, and one confused teenager dressed like a dog on his way to a breakout at the pound. Poor old Buster got hauled in for animal abuse and disturbing the peace. Dog was not surprisingly made magistrate so Buster got off with a very light sentence.

Lost Gnosis

Wow, it says here we are bits and pieces of a star! Reading on, a bit is anywhere from one to under a hundred parts. A piece is a hundred parts or more. (On page seven of our manual.) Over years, a bit can grow, become a piece or many bits can get together after their last supper and turn into a piece in seconds, make hit news. It's still a question (page fourteen) whether pieces from single bits over time or from bits joined together after the dessert wine are the way to go. What's not important is that all of us can knock an eye out with our whitest teeth or drive circles around our greenest neighbors. Of consequence is grace, the ridding of all vestments from our persons, the fullest widening of gaps among our atoms. (Whew, okay, next to the last page.) When what we used to walk on becomes water and there'll be no deserts ever, all our questions will be answers, including what parts are. (Back to page seven.) Wait, pages are no longer! No matter.

Raising

Pop wonders how I can look at the barn, his grandfather's barn and now our barn and not see its trees, hundreds felled, debarked and dredged, cut into beam lengths, posts, chisel-squared, mortised, hand-drilled for pegs whittled from twigs and I, who've never even seen a tree but in pictures, make up some song and dance that the barn most likely arrived pre-cut and assembled. I tell Pop I can picture the workers at the factory: former circus clowns, knife throwers, a host of strong men and bearded ladies putting in their shifts until they had one barn ready for pickup or delivery. No way had there been good ole neighbor boys with horses and hammers, no way no faithful wives with casseroles, jugs of tea. Just an A gone into B, a C squared off with D, then one big lumbered roll of a drum and *BARN!*

Tree?

Jack's out working the ground when he bumps into a tree. What's a tree doing here and there appears to be no way around it but Jack's really got to get to the other side to keep working, the alternative being spend the night, future nights on this side but he's been on this side way too long as the overworked ground will attest so he climbs up this sunny side of the tree, scratching notes on his forearm as he goes about the thinness of branches, thickness of leaves, the ratios of birds to insects and insects to seeds, the presence or absence of marsupials and the views, always the views, how what's down below gets farther away the higher up he goes until he reaches the treetop itself where everything's the very farthest and he begins his descent down the trunk's shady bark, similar but still opposite of what he climbed up and then, then he's down, down on the kissable ground where he turns to discover this was never a tree at all but the biggest oldest bean stalk around.

Big Game

Amos pitched a potato over the shed roof and, in seconds, it came flying back. He was simply trying to get rid of it, not play catch. He walked around to the opposite side but saw nobody there. Then Amos tried a nice turnip. Same thing as the potato but much more colorful on return, more like a living planet than an asteroid. Lastly Amos decided to shot put a cabbage. Over the roof it flew, big like the moon and it too came barreling back, shredding itself on re-entry. Worms and grubs ate what they could and quickly grew way out of proportion into a second string team. They eventually made their way to the other side of the shed where they took down Axel, the wolf spider quarterback.

Tale of Three Thumbs

Tom agrees everyone, no matter what, should have a thumb. One at least, preferably two, and even a spare in a vacuum-sealed bottle in the knife drawer. A thumb should be opposable or else it's only good as a toe. Tom's buddy Ben has an opposable toe which he uses to pick up loose change on the sidewalk. Ben just isn't human, some neighbors say, but what then? A damn good cheat at cards, my pop says. Tom lost his thumb years ago playing chicken. A doctor with special tools and terrific thumbs himself attached a new thumb onto Tom's stub. Offhand, I'd like to know when a stub can still be a thumb. Reeney the manicurist says when it's still got some nail left, some nail you can file, some nail you can enamel and buff. Two months ago Tom found his old thumb he's not telling where so now he's got three! He keeps it in a matchbox in the freezer next to those popsicles only he knows the flavor of.

Straight Shooting

I'm surprised I'm even writing this down, you see Brock was telling me in his pickup this afternoon he'd like to take out Gil next weekend and I got a little rush and urged him on by saying 'bout time somebody did and Brock turned to me while scratching his head, almost running us into the culvert over by the trade school as he soon set me straight by saying, on a date, dickhead, on a date, not blow his brains out with the double barrel and I tell Brock no matter what you do, one way or the other, Gil ain't gonna know what hit him.

End of the Line

One morning I got on the bus to go someplace but forgot where so I rode to the end of the line and the driver made me get off and then made me pay to get back on so I took my good ole time fishing in my pocket for exact change which set him off schedule by nearly six minutes which he didn't seem too worked about until this big crow flew into his windshield, guts and glass all over the front seats which I agreed to help clean up with a broom and some rags and fortunately it was a beautiful spring day, come to think of it, the first day of spring and at the first return stop, everyone getting on was resetting his watch and on each stop after, resetting again so when we pulled in to the last stop downtown at the drugstore across from the old post office now the county lockup, everyone was late for work and the bus driver got off and walked but I stayed on and drove the bus to the bus windshield repair shop whose bus windshield repairman shook his head as he scratched it: crows, right? Damn crows.

Secret Door

Every house has one. It often opens up into a secret room, usually empty but sometimes not. Sometimes the secret room holds objects never imagined, objects that dazzle, objects that make unearthly sounds and these objects remain with the room, the owner cannot sell them or throw them out, they must remain like the walls or windows just where they are but then sometimes a secret door simply leads to a room used all the time and the door is there for convenience like aiding in disappearing at a party or letting a dog out that was never the owner's to begin with. Often the secret door appears like it's part of the wall, doesn't want recognition but then sometimes it screams *D O O R* and wants to be in charge of all the other doors in the house from trap door to front door and it's there at the front door where trouble often starts. No door, secret or otherwise, tells the front door what to do. Well, maybe the back door does but that requires a whole other opening.

Two

Stu went out last night with a blond bombshell. No, really!
No one was more surprised than the bombshell.

Brads

All over the country Brads are repeatedly falling in love with themselves, in storefronts, in chrome bumpers of parked cars, chasing after chrome bumpers of speeding cars, in ladies' compact mirrors briefly flipped open for touch-ups, in wide mirrors of trailering dualies, in shiny new quarters whose reflections could not distort Brads' superbly chiseled corners, all thirty-two hundred teeth, kaleidoscope irises that dazzle, yes, Brads have it all but are giving all up with each grip of themselves in something reflective that's really not reflective at all but absorbent, a thief in the night light that does not, cannot, would not give back if it could.

Man in Blue

A little girl serves imaginary oolong tea to a once-thought humble bear in her bedroom. Older brother appears by formal, non-refusable invitation of the mother. Word's out older brother wants to run all three over with his little truck, leave them splinters.

Tea pretends to cool. The low watt in the easy-bake oven is raising a last tart. Mr. Bear is losing patience. He's hungry, finds the missing sibling shaking in the refrigerator. He calls a cop who's been waiting months to meet the mother, both now divorced.

The cop installs an imaginary siren in the older brother's little truck. He points Mr. Bear toward a hive. He gives the little tea server something silver from his pocket. And wraps the little fridge shaker in an electric blanket that he'll carry with him through life.

Farmer's Daughter

Candace stepped out with this cornstalk from the neighboring field, one the neighboring harvester had missed. It whispered its name, she couldn't repeat or spell it but it did bring a smile and that was enough for Candace so one day she and the cornstalk went on a picnic, danced through the crow-littered stubble, the two of them as described by our neighbors actually looked like a double, Candace herself mostly skin and bone but it was the shadows, or should I say shadow, they cast in the harvest moonlight that convinced us they'd already become one.

Name on It

Some folks are satisfied to write a book, some to have a street named after them, but Jasper wants an ocean or continent, some huge mass alive with life and it's own colors and patterns, its own time zones, its own food chain and then's when John, Jasper's best friend and the only one with a planetary pole named after him, has to bring Jasper to his senses so John pummels him in the neck with his bowling ball and when Jasper gets up from the gutter, he rolls a perfect strike and the first perfect game of the evening and sees his name, *J A S P E R*, everyone sees it blinking on the marquee outside on the roof and traffic on the exit coming off the interstate is congesting where the noise has become unbearable and I ask Jasper if this is what he wants and he says, nope, but close enough.

T-Day

November, near its end when Terry told of fighting off a flock of wild turkeys out on the lawn near the stump where men with saws and axes had harvested the ash, had it on the ground in no time and here was where I did not know the turkeys roosted to watch the neighbor kids play ball, poor though they were, pitch old potatoes from the neighbor's field his dog dug up and when some kid would get a hit, the turkeys gobbled like a cheering stand of fans and flapped their wings so hard the leaves shook, fell, did not come back come spring, any spring, the tree had died and had to be brought down, it's stand of wild turkeys unforgiving until each feller took a turkey home hoping a connection might be made, perhaps a friendship but as we know, the tables turned when everyone sat down, said grace.

Kissin' Cous

Jethro is living the dream, my other cousin remarks, just look at him there in his cowboy pajamas with his duel cap pistols in their holsters, his getting tripped up in his own little lasso and is that tobacco juice real and what I'd give for a buckaroo hat like the one he keeps slapping dust out of on his leatherette chaps. The trick is he's sleepwalking and even when I tell him after he wakes up, he tells me I'm full of it, that I've been swallowing too much tobacco juice and he's right, Jethro's a genius or a genie and I've always believed everything about him, even those hugs and kisses with his eyes closed.

So Definitive

Marty was leafing through his dictionary, I knew it was his because he'd written *Marty* on every page and when I asked what he was looking up, he said he was trying to put together the simplest declarative sentence and up till now he'd constructed everything but and I asked if he even had an inkling of what he wanted to declare and he snidely asked me when I'd become a customs agent and I said, no, no, you've got it all wrong and he said, that's what all my teachers tell me and I want to shock them with something so definitive, he had to look that up by the way, they'll all faint from embarrassment and so he creates this sentence of twenty-six words, each begun with a letter of the alphabet in alphabetical order and when he read it to me, it made no sense but his quantum physics teacher called his preacher and told him Marty's just said in one sentence all there was to say about the nature of consciousness and its survival after the death of the body and the preacher said he'd be willing to use it in his sermon, will even post it on the big church billboard by the exit ramp so long as it's in the form of a question.

Cold Season

Mac was telling me that when he was a young snot nose he used to go to this bar where all the other young snot noses in town went and they'd have bugger-flicking contests, not a lot unlike darts and of course the assholes who had had colds for a week had the advantage until one night Mac says, he recalls it being a Tuesday, lots of rain on the sidewalks outside, this young skinny whippersnapper sloshes into the bar and offers a challenge, not picking and flicking but snorting one nostril at a time and no one knew what the hell he was talking about until he gave a demonstration and his singular string of snot pretty much ejaculated across the bar like an arrow, fortunately for him and those standing close, not like a boomerang, and landed on the moose head Ole Pete the original proprietor bagged years ago in some woods up north and of course everyone sipping whatever it was they were sipping were taken aback and hauled ass off the stools and now nobody found their fingers in the party mix so the place closed way before closing and a good thing too because that very night, the cops were going to come down hard and nobody would be spared so Mac's buddy Carl, so Mac tells it, lit a fart and the place went up in flames just like it read next day in the paper, well, damn near.

Garage Man

Horace from down the block who lives part-time in his garage talks of nothing but his tools, particularly those whose painted shadows grace the pegboard. Last earthquake when they shook and swayed upon their hooks, he just happened to record their sounds and, I must say, gave Phillip Glass a run for his money and Mike Oldfield, the Tubular Bells guy and the organ grinder's monkey, the one on the corner of Fifth and Birch, not the one near the dry cleaner nor the one behind Wendy's, so when push showed up as shove, Horace jacked up his garage and mounted wheels on its footers and hit the road Jack, it is Jack I'm telling this to, correct, so Horace hits the road, clanging along for everyone in the county with intentions to clang the whole nation and nice thing about it all was if anything broke down along the way, Horace had the tools to fix it so long as it did not require anesthesia but unfortunately never make it better, even a little better than what it was and this lack of improvement and/or innovation was Horace's downfall and when he finally got back home, he pulled his rig over right across the street from me, me who he visits every day now that I've shown him my vastly superior collection of tuning forks, not to mention the set of silver spoons my great grandfather played mostly at his favorite bar and a wedding here and there, articles have been written about him and them and Horace tells me he can't sleep anymore without dreaming of all that silver so I let him sleep part-time in my garage so long as he remembers to pick up after himself and pull the door down when he leaves, hmm, if he leaves.

Coat

Trent went to the thrift and tried on a coat. It fit him to a tee but he hated the collar. Some tall guy tried it on but hated the buttons. A young girl twirled in it until she heard laughter, then put it back on the rack. Trent grabbed it again. This time he loved it, he loved every facet and the coat loved him back so he took it. Trent and his coat went out for some take-out, it looked pretty starved and then they went for an airing. When they got home, Trent couldn't take it off. A note in the pocket read he had to die first.

To Test

For the last half hour Benny's been belting himself in the driver's seat with his head positioned precisely above the middle of the steering wheel. He's got on his hard hat with visor to divert at least a little of any flying glass. He's trying really hard to let his limbs go limp so as to lessen the effects of dashboard impact. And he's got a full bladder just in case there might be sparks. He's wrapped the rearview mirror's rosary twice around his left hand and has inserted the plastic dashboard Jesus tightly in the makeshift scabbard of his right sleeve. With the radio tuned to all gospel all the time, last check on his checklist, he's finally in position to test for the crash dummy post at the plant.

Three Drops

It rained three drops last night and here they are. On the windowsill. Look. They are unlike anything you've ever seen, practically beyond description. Go ahead, try, share what you see with anyone listening but meanwhile, let's not disturb them. They've traveled who knows how far and for how long. They've captured who knows what that's now inside them or on their surfaces, invisible to the naked eye, invisible even under the strongest microscope. I'm just guessing but maybe they're just resting, not being absorbed by anything, not evaporating into thin air, not even reflecting. They're just here on the windowsill. Until they're not.

Aerosol Age

Sam went out of his way to avoid me. The anti-Sam aerosol I sprayed on myself this morning was working! I'd found it in the pest section at the Walmart, the one over on Regal. Which reminds me, I need to get some anti-Cindy for my wife. Cindy, as you might have guessed, is Sam's latest in an impressive spreadsheet of squeezes. Oh look, here comes Herbert and I'm immediately pushed out of his way. He must have on his anti-Gary. I know that because I'm Gary and I suddenly feel a bit woozy and have to sit down on the little folding stool I carry around with me anymore. While I rest and revive, I reflect on the old days when we could just tell each other what was on our minds, shake hands or not and be done with it.

Night Rider

Virgil rides his bike at night in the street when there are no cars. If there is no moon, he ties a big white balloon on a long string to his seat post. Lights from the lamp posts and nearby houses make it shine. He doesn't stay out long and just before he comes back in, he pops the balloon with the safety pin that holds up his pants. His pants fall down. Dogs start to bark and lights blink on. He pins his pants back up, chains his bike up and floats off to bed. Dogs quiet down and lights blink off. Virgil dreams he is home.

Three

All the way to town Jeff wrestled with the steering wheel
until the air bag went off and pinned him,
so the story went and got misplaced on the sports page.

Window over the Sink

This morning I watched my neighbor Evelyn leave her house to go to work when she walked right past her little Corolla on the curb and got into the neighbors' parked behind their garage. Eventually the neighbors caught her through their window over the sink and I could see them from mine and waved and of course they could see me and waved back. After an hour or so I looked out and Evelyn's still sitting there. I got to wondering what was going on so I put on my hat and coat, went out and knocked on the window. She mumbled something to me over the tick and hum. This was no car at all but the time machine I'd heard was in the neighborhood. I remembered the bookmobile was due any day and the bloodmobile expected Thursday so when she told me through her now rolled-down window her fondest desire was to go to a brand new place and time with me in them, what else could I do but hop in.

Joy Ride

Axel liked to stand on his car roof and pee down the windshield. His friend Bumper would then turn on the wipers and run them on intermittent. Neither ever told anyone. It was just something they did. Upon speculation one might reason they needed a break from their chores. Or they simply liked taking turns and, if you remember, Bumper peed down the windshield last time. Anyhow, next time they planned on simply coasting down the street as neighbors were hosing down their driveways. Then out onto a bumpy country road where the deer on the shoulder would stop chomping and look up, surely shake their heads and make that tsk-tsk sound with their exceptional tongues. Then Axel and Bumper would pull over for pick-me-ups at Rix's Quik Fix Diner and if Rix's waitress looked old enough to drive with or without a license and would be ending her shift soon, they might ask her if she'd like to ride along.

Local Physics

All over Newtonville folks are jumping from high places. Ike witnessed two come down off a house roof, sixteen, oops there's two more, make that eighteen from some treetops, dodging branch after branch after branch. Ike also knew each jump from high places was intended, for once again, old gravity just had to be tested and those of us not in doubt of invisible forces just fell out of bed and went off to work. The real miracle here is not one jumper died. One moment they were up at the top, next moment flailing through the air like a swimmer out of water, lastly simply walking away with ne'er a hair out of place and if you ask any of them, they always defer to some character in a cartoon famed for its multitudinous lives: the miracle mouse, the courageous coyote, the honeybee-chased bear who routinely show up next episode as grounded as when each first drew breath.

Make of Him

Jack went just like that overnight, can you believe it, yesterday a welder with his rods and his torch and this morning, has found himself making up bouquets in wicker baskets at the Food Circus, even the cart hustlers are snickering for here's this hunk of a man who exchanged his asbestos apron for a flimsy poly wraparound and petal stains on his once-singed fingers. No one knew what to make of him, even after he explained he saw this coming in all those myriad sparks, you see he said he needed living color and a flurry of shapes and a platform where he still could get his hands and apron dirty so today everyone, even the men, who now come in to shop remarked how Jack's eyes sparkled, what a beautiful smile, and a chin he could chisel mountains with but for Jack, it became all about smell now that he'd discovered things he could.

Dirty Dancin'

Lois likes to visit the laundromat early as do about forty other dirty-clothes hounds to feel, as she describes, the place take off: five quarters per machine slid into place, the rush of water entering the tubs, local air suffused with suds, floor tiles rattling upon their concrete substrates with everybody, I mean everybody on their feet, Lois in the middle, then out the door and into the street where rhythms are residual but still felt just enough to know the dirtiest among them will eventually, or maybe never, come clean.

Pick Ups

Ellis pulled an empty shopping cart from its corral in the parking lot, rolled into the store and immediately headed over to Lane One where he picked up one of everything from the impulse-purchase shelves and loaded in his cart, then placed each item on the conveyor belt which the cashier scanned and bagged, then Ellis put all the bags into his cart and bee-lined over to Customer Service where he told the representative none of the items were what he really wanted, a few too big, a few too small, several were missing parts, and the remainder he couldn't remember what they were even for and now he'd simply like to return them for a credit so the representative whose tag read Lois or Louise, he couldn't be sure, unloaded his cart and handed him a credit, then Ellis rolled on over to Lane Two and impulse-purchased again, checked out and headed back to Customer Service, got another credit from someone named Mary or Marcy, he couldn't be sure and headed for Lane Three and so on and so on until the Customer Service Manager named Annabelle printed very clearly on her tag saw Ellis pushing toward her with his loaded cart and before he even opened his mouth, she said okay, okay, I'll go out with you. Pick me up at seven. Don't bring anything.

The Six-Foot Man

He tries to follow the rules so every time he's out in the stores, in an aisle or at checkout, he gets down on his hands and knees and stretches out on the floor where someone accidentally steps on his toes while someone else trips over his head, causing his little blue mask to come off, his consciousness now on the line so he calls for the manager to come manage which doesn't include helping him get up but the manager does offer a job lying down wherever safe distancing is in question, even selects a sharp uniform, hard hat from stock as shoppers now dangerously crowd one another just to see him lie down on the job as they chuckle and applaud all together, plan to surely come back next week, many more after this.

More of Itself

We'd gone to the park, my friend Josh and I just to sit and stare at the trees because somebody staring at us on the subway told us we might catch them living their lives, they'd been living their lives for decades, centuries through thick and thin, sunshine and rain, sleet and hail but, the subway-staring somebody said, try to catch them in the act, try to see in just one sitting mere fractions of their actual living, so Josh and I went and sat, sat sat and more sat for one entire afternoon and not one tree, not one twig had advanced by a millimeter nor by a millimeter of a millimeter either upward or outward so Josh and I climbed up on one of the branches and looked down for the bench we'd been sitting on and there it was, three hundred pounds lighter, there it was making more of itself, becoming a little amphitheater on the edge of the park, all happening so fast like we didn't see a thing, like it'd been there all along and ever would be.

The Moon

Over and over and over again I keep thinking how the moon does it since it hasn't got a brain as far as neurologists know and no real desire with a capital D as far as psychologists know, hasn't got a pilot as far as air traffic controllers know and yet it's up there night after night looking down wide-eyed or peeking and winking at me for no reason other than flirtation, sharing thoughts of temperature, of rock and dust and lesser gravity and my near invisibility with its five i's, each with its own little moon and I try to explain to the big moon the romance we humans and a few howling hounds have with it in song but it's not moved, nor I, frozen here on the hood of my pickup in Target's parking lot at three in the morning, scratching raw confessions in the windshield's blue frost.

Dream Boat

Running underneath the porch last night, I know, you're gonna say those two old possums but no, it was a small creek and docked near the front stoop was a small boat, small creek small boat, get it, and a couple of oars, so me and my significant other crawl down through the floorboards and get in, oh, and it's surprisingly bright down here like it has its own moon so we row, first under the porch that leads into the basement past the Ping-Pong table that thinks it's a pool table and washer that thinks it's a dryer, then out the outside basement door where we find ourselves in mangy Maine on a mini-vacation like last fall when the leaves just started to turn and now we've hit some rapids, hold on there honeybunch, hold on, and I get us through and next thing we know, we're in dry dock, sitting four feet off the ground still in our boat across a couple of two-by-sixes where a few neighbors have gathered, pointing and laughing and we point and laugh too, it must look pretty funny when just then news of the dam breaking comes over the air waves, we read the headlines in the cirrus sky and our neighbors are suddenly washed away in the current but me and my significant other are lifted up to our second floor window where we climb in and crawl into bed. Next time, me and my significant other can't sleep, we've agreed to cups of warm milk and some star gazing, only the ones gazing back with love in their eyes, of course.

American Field Days

Farmer Dan wanted to make room in the crib for the new ears so every day he tossed a bushel or so of old ears into a pen where whitetail, turkey, and bear could get through and eat and within days Farmer Dan had a sizeable, both in number and girth, wild herd he was hoping to harness in some way to help harvest the new crop and all was going along jimdandily until the whitetail, turkey, and bear got into the crib of new ears as well, they had a field day which turned into a field week and in no time, a cross-county event with tractor pulls and ribbon pinnings and the best funnel cakes anywhere in Corncrib County where Farmer Dan patented the petting zoo with franchises as far away as Saskatchewan but he never moved there, never even paid a visit.

Paper Opera

The man in the square has his head in the comics. I know this because I am nursing an orange popsicle on the limb above him and a little to his left. A tragedy of a woman going by flicks her Ginny Slim, sets the Bumsteads on fire! Blondie feels the heat and takes steps two at a time to stir Dagwood asleep in the tub. Daisy keeps tugging on Mr. Beasley's mailbag. Alexander and Cookie rush back from the mall. The man can't believe it when I let my popsicle drip down into the Bumsteads' foyer. The fire is out! There's a hole in the paper now and through it past his knees to the right of his toes are ashes from Blondie's coat tree and carved teak umbrella urn. The man reaches down to pick something up. Adds spit. Makes a paste. Patches the hole. He gets up and goes, leaves the paper on the bench. The woman is long gone from the tinkling boy fountain. I leave the elm and enter adulthood. The Bumsteads and their neighbors tornado down the block, over toes, over grass, under some flowers. Multi-nations hold their breaths for the morning edition: not even Mr. Dithers makes the obits.

Jim's Wind

Out of the blue my buddy Jim whispers to me he can see wind, not just any wind but *the* wind and I'm more than a little shaken as Jim's been blind since birth so what's it look like, *the* wind, I ask and he says like his hand, the one he doesn't write with, only bigger, much bigger, maybe as big as his whole body and it waves, sometimes a hello wave, sometimes a goodbye and sometimes like someone on the tail end of drowning and sometimes it looks like it's just telling a nice story like hula dancers do with their hands and then I ask Jim what he saw the wind hand doing yesterday and Jim begins to cry as he says it slapped him silly as if to wake him from a deep deep sleep, warn him, make him forever wary of what's always around the corner, something not even someone with 20/20 can see coming and weeks after, I hear others are seeing wind too, I tell Jim I can see it in their eyes so I don't have to ask but not everyone we discover sees wind as a hand, some see it as a wing, some as a wand and I tell Jim what a lucky man he is as I and much of the world can't see wind at all, only what it does, what it leaves in its wake and then Jim asks me out of the blue what I see when I see him and I tell him not just any wind. Jim's.

Words Have to Do

My neighbor Brick was in his backyard putting together this palace of a playhouse for his sweet little princess and obviously needed someone to hold the timbers in place while he bolted them together with silver nuts and bolts. After four hours the playhouse was up just as his little princess arrived home from preschool, her eyes, bigger and brighter than the bolt parts themselves, and she continued to run all gleeful-like in circles before collapsing into her pooped-out daddy's waiting arms, then she picked up his adjustable and shook it at me, said, scram daddy-o! all with that little twinkle in her eye, said, you're remaining presence is dulling the magic so I gave her a little wink and a nose tweak just before the playhouse folded itself up and got back in its box, leaving little princess with king daddy Brick dethroned upon the sod. Believe me, I'd have taken pictures had I film.

I Heard

Black bear with missing teeth meets face to face with old buck, half his rack gone.

That you Herb? asks black bear with missing teeth.

You bet your jawbone, Hal. This past year's been hell, hell on wheels, pickup-truck-full-of-outlaws hell. Know what I mean?

Hey, scratch my back, will you Herb?

Sure, if you'll help me hold my head up while I maneuver through this underbrush.

How's that, Herb?

Much better, Hal.

So where do we go from here? asks Hal.

To the ridge where I heard apples and plums are already on the ground. Nobody knows how they got there. No trees around.

Let's beat a path fast, if you can make it, says Herb.

I can if you can, snaps back Hal. Let's hope when we get there, it's all true.

No Good Deed

When Tim was getting dressed one morning he heard someone yelling for help so he ran outside buck naked, then down the street still hearing *help, help*, ran all the way to town ignoring his hurting feet, seeing no one anywhere, then tried the doors of shops and finally entered one that sold men's clothing, no one inside where he slipped on pants, a shirt, new shoes then went outside where *help, help* was still in the air so when he came upon a little dog yelping and yelping that sounded like *help, help*, Tim picked her up and calmed her down and both were happy when it was over but soon police came running down the street, shaking their clubs, accusing Tim of multiple crimes: indecent exposure, breaking and entering, theft, cruelty to animals and downright poor taste. Tim confessed. If only he'd remembered his wife Alice's words: never a red shirt with green pants dear, even if it's Christmas. Fortunately Tim was let go with a pocketful of warnings and Alice let him keep his new little Princess.

County Highway 409

Out on County Highway 409 a chimpanzee is on a ten-speed. No one gets excited about a chimpanzee on a ten-speed out on County Highway 409. The chimpanzee is not all over the road. He pretty much keeps to the middle on the yellow line. Anyone passing can easily go by him even when two pass at once but every now and then, someone gets cocky and forces the chimpanzee onto the shoulder where he always regains his composure for that's what shoulders are for, then maneuvers back to the middle to pick up where he left off. Thing is, a few folks living out on County Highway 409 believe the chimpanzee's really the sheriff still stuck inside his old parade costume so they toss him frosted cupcakes as he rides by so long as he flashes his badge.

Plugs

After weeks of hem-hawing around, I finally got an email off to the maker of my spongy little plugs, complaining they're not at all what I had heard them to be. Yes, it's true I barely hear any engine noise when I'm mowing, TV or radio when I'm trying to sleep but the thing is I've begun to pick up sounds from the plugs themselves like they've absorbed rather than deflected what they're meant to keep out and then play them back at the most inconvenient times, even playing them in conjunction with sounds that seep in in real time and every now and then I will admit, this collaboration is defyingly brilliant, beyond Bach, beyond the Beatles, beyond Frippertronics! I wish you could hear what I hear but your instructions do not recommend sharing, it being unsanitary and all unless, unless I let them harden into something like talc, then pulverize them into a fine dust, each mote now a note and let wind whisper them out over the lawns and then what? We'd be back where we started with hearing what's for some, overbearing and their utterly needing your plugs and hey, hey mister plug maker, it was your plan all along, wasn't it? Wasn't it?

Borderland

Kenny with his camera asks me what I've got there and I hold up one blue spruce, one Norway spruce, a white pine, and a jack pine, all dirt cheap from Lonny's Lawn and Garden that I'm going to plant where my backyard meets the woods so I say, lose the camera Kenny, grab a shovel, help me dig four nice deep holes but first we have to move the stones I'd laid down long ago and in a few short hours, the spruces and the pines are in, four little conifers in otherwise deciduous soil. Months later Kenny without his camera comes to visit so we take a walk to see the trees we'd set, each having taken on the shape and stance of its dog beneath, Kenny knows it wasn't me who did this, me who could not shape or shave a tree to save a life nor turn it into something it was not although I did learn how to bring a statue back to life one summer in the park but here we both stood among our flourishing green pups on their paths to full-fledged fragrant Fidos as we ourselves stood fading.

Four

Even when you're holding your own hand,
there will be times you'll have to let go.

My Father as Car

Buick imported Opels in 1972 when I was in grad school and my dad paid $2772 for my beautiful blue Manta that I took to Ohio where it got pelletted by hail during a tornado and I drove through a Nationwide drive-thru and got an instant check which I used to live on while I drove my dimpled baby for ten more years and my dad never asked to be paid back but I gave back years of grace instead and would do it again and again because that's what good sons do when Buick gives up Opels and you can't get parts even if you find a mechanic who'd replace them for you so I buy a Jetta, another German make, this one assembled in Mexico that my father never saw except from a distance one always thought was vast but finds out later is only inches away and I discovered he took it for a drive one night because I found it facing in the opposite direction next morning, keys above the visor, tank empty.

Billy as Tree

Bill tells his son Billy to gather the leaves so Billy's out there with glue tacking them back on the tree but a whole lot get stuck to his fingers, eyebrows, his elbows, his knees so Billy spreads more glue, rolls in the pile, is making himself into a tree and he's soon in the neighbor's yard, the neighbor blowing his leaves so Billy makes his arms move like branches, his fingers like twigs but what to do with his head sticking out so he thinks like a tree and bows it.

Spree

Look. Count 'em. Sixteen buff mannequins standing at the bus stop where the bus driver is shouting out the door to anyone of them, there must be a live one somewhere among you but not a one moves, and after nearly ten minutes when the driver has wrenched exact change out of each of their cracked, flaking fingers, everyone is finally on board on their way to the abandoned mall.

No Need for Intros

There were maybe six of us on the whole of Main. A warm morning. No one was running. Only one couple glued at the hip and shoulders. Not one stray. Everyone simply went on their way. Nobody waved or shouted, "Nice morning." Then I stopped for no reason. Perhaps to get a reaction. Everyone surprisingly stopped too. Nothing inched except eyeballs. To the left, then the right, up, then down like in an eye exam. I pointed to the sky. I opened my mouth in a long, silent O. Everyone did likewise. I shook my fist like I was mad at a cloud. It wasn't the bully cloud that had been blocking the sun but a little gassy one that had been trying to get by. The air quickly filled with raised fists. Windows of apartments above stores opened up with raised fists. All of a sudden the little cloud caught fire brought on by the friction of fists. It fell on us like ash from a backyard burn barrel. We rubbed it on our hands and faces, our bare arms. We were just happy to have pigment again.

All It Takes

Steve and I are sitting out in the backyard. It's nearly dark when he asks me, what's that bulge there in your pocket, and I tell him, oh, that's the moon. Yeh, right, he sneers, really, what is it and I squeeze it out without getting up, you see I'd just sat down, and hold it in my hand. He wants to touch it but he's afraid. He blows on it, sniffs it and finally pokes it where it makes a little sound like a start of song and then I ask him, are you done, and he says, sure, okay. I tell him I want to go and hang it in the sweet gum tree that parts our yards and as I'm reaching up, he spots me just in case I teeter or it gets too heavy but it never does.

Sweet Potato

Clean men are not men. Dirty men, men of grit, men of grime are men, men who leave work and walk home like they're in a parade, never on it. They withdraw into night's dark, become it with no daylight in sight. The good earth smells of them and their dark dirt remains on my palm after a handshake. I wash it, save the dirty water for the sweet potato stuck with toothpicks on the sill. Before long, its leaves will curtain the window; its roots, break the jar.

Always Room

Day is coming to a close, as well the cemetery, whose gate being locked I'm still skinny enough to squeeze through into the lives registered and remembered in granite and marble, when over the grass a haze is beginning, then congesting into more of a fog, one with a whiff of cigarettes and cigarillos, pipes large and small, including the one packed with pot in my shirt pocket I share with my buddy passed on, both of us rising with thought and affection so dense I am no longer able to see him, sense him, but the taste of his breath on its way to my lungs, their little limbs hugging my heart when I find myself nodding off on his sod, his twin bed which could double for two, did many nights at our start, does and will do so long as we continue to thin.

Five

Loaves not shared are stubble.

Show's Almost Over

Archie is slowly unbecoming a ventriloquist. This sort of thing doesn't happen overnight. It could take weeks, even years, but right now he's sitting on his dummy's lap and reciting some stale but not necessarily tasteless one-liners and if you watch closely, you'll see the dummy's lips move hardly at all and it sounds like Archie sounding like a parrot and when he's all done, he tries to fold himself up in his suitcase while the dummy is hypnotizing hangers-on in the front row of seats who are down on their knees pecking at dropped popcorn from a year ago when the joint was a movie theater and the butter, lip-smackin', I do mean lip-smackin' good.

Into a Corner

I tell my friend Pat he's a scaredy cat and he wonders what the hell I'm going on about. See the rug in your room, see where it's worn? I ask. You leave an obvious path to your bed, one to your wardrobe, one to the window, but none, not a fraction of wear to a corner, any corner. It can hardly be fear as you don't know if there's anything in any corner to be afraid of and it can't be a waste of time, of footsteps because you haven't done anything to prove or disprove either so what is it, Pat? Are you waiting for someone to take you by the hand, to kick you in the rear, to lure you with a promise of a good time? No? So you just need to make up your mind to go there. It won't, can't take more than a minute and I'll wait right here in the doorway for you to come back, that's if you do, just kidding, and if the walls do close in on you like you're bologna between two slices of white, I'll pull you out and I'll want a good story for others to hear what led you to do such a goofball thing as walk yourself into a corner and only a select few of the tabloid readers will ask why that corner when there were three others and do you have plans to walk into them at some point as well. Just know, from where I stand here in this doorway, the very same I stood in last aftershock, you are a true pioneer among pioneers and deserve to be jotted down on a Post-It of history, Pat. Pat, are you listening? Pat? Where are you, Pat?

To the Shoes

Dana's opened a shoe store on her front porch where there were once potted plants and life-sized knick-knacks, these I can only imagine now sit out in the rain off the back porch but let's go back out front before a crowd gathers because what Dana's put out there is nothing less than kick-ass, I mean colors and shapes and sizes until now only known outside the state, you can only guess which, and as the light and temperature change throughout the day, these shoes move, they step up and dance, they make their own music, I'm not kidding, they click their heels and point their toes and tap and spin around like tops and my mind being mine can only think of the legs that once ended in these shoes, long lean legs with the tautest of calves and shapeliest of thighs, legs that lifted high over heads, flinging what once cost a week's pay into a crowd who'd also forgotten until Dana's opening.

Oranges

Oh I know, there must be dozens of varieties from all over the world, you holding in your weary, war-torn palm one sweeter, one more sun-kissed, one oranger than your neighbor's, your forefinger and thumb peeling back rind, zest zesting out in every cardinal direction, then you're pulling a section, pushing it between lips where you show it like happy sad teeth, juice trickling down your chin, neck, inside your shirt, flooding your navel and belly trenches and all of a sudden your whole head is an orange and all of your round parts turn into oranges and your feet squish as you march down the avenue right up until the moment you stick and passersby rush to lick what's left off your chin and not only yours but orange chins everywhere until the thirst of the whole planet is quenched.

Bobbing Dead

Jim adopts this old dog, some kind of spaniel-beagle mix. He never wanted a purebred, never liked their dispositions, their genetically predetermined behaviors. Anyway, old Bosco dies shortly after Jim gets him but instead of Jim burying him in the backwoods by the tree where he liked to tree squirrels, Jim takes him to Jack, his taxidermist friend who also has degrees in mechanical engineering and voice. A week or so later Jim takes new Bosco home. He carries him from room to room to room, in and out of the house but never to town because old Bosco always hated the hustle bustle and would want to crawl inside Jim's coat. Come one Tuesday Jim finds new Bosco gone. Jim knows he probably should have just put him in the ground. At least he would have known where he was! Meanwhile Jim gets this call from Todd himself down at Todd's TVs telling him new Bosco's outside on the sidewalk watching all sixteen screens through the big plate glass window and now he's rolling over, now up on hind legs, now up on front legs, now chasing his tail, now singing what sounds like a cover from Abba. I'm on my way, Jim says. Next stop, the auditions.

No Joke

A red, a yellow, and a blue party balloon escaped out of a bar. Actually they were let out when a customer walked in. They flew higher than a kite and together became a dot. Only me and a crow watched until it was gone, then looked into each others' eyes, harder for me as the crow's were on the sides of his head. Crow squawked he could still see all three balloons in my eyes and I explained memory to him because he didn't seem to have one. Within minutes he'd retrieved some balloon animals a party planner up on the bar roof had twisted into shapes. Crow was so happy to have friends again to play with that he went flying around with them for hours, showing them his favorite fields and backyards and a watery spot down by the dump. Talk around town now was everyone wanted a balloon on a string with a crow attached and asked where I got mine. I told them I couldn't remember ever having a balloon or string or a crow and that they just might have had one too many.

The Standing

Roger tells anybody who asks that he is just standing by the window. Still as a post. Not looking out. Not listening to trees. Not listening to bees. And not stopping breathing so there's no need to worry. He hates having to repeat this to passersby who ask. For six seconds he contemplates making a sign but he knows this will only encourage more questions leading to full-blown conversations, then dates for coffee and more talk over lunches and by then he'd have been sitting down for hours when all he ever wanted was to stand for as long as he could stand standing. Know what I mean? he says. Those were his last words to date. Oh, he sits and lies down some now and then but always goes back to standing. He even sleeps standing most of the time. Once I saw him with his arms out and his fingers spread, bare toes spread too. He looked just like the ash in his backyard before it was brought down. Except it didn't have a head sticking out. Or maybe it did. Nobody can remember.

Great Whale

Once in a great whale, I mean while, okay, let's stick with whale for awhile so I decide to look around but it's dark so I strike the match I always carry in my shirt pocket and light the candle I always carry inside my sock, something my older brother always did as well, I never asked why so here I am inside this great whale, how I got in the ocean to begin with I'd like to know, I hate the water, never learned to swim so I guess as long as I remain inside this great whale, I'll be fine but the candle eventually burns down and I'm afraid of the dark and say so and the great whale hears me and everything I've heard about whales, great or not so, is they're gentle and smart so this great whale amps up his power station, whatever and wherever that is, and his insides become a veritable ballroom where I've got the whole floor to myself, Paul Winter is blowing his slender sax and the great whale is accompanying and I am swooning, hopefully for a little whale, I mean while, longer.

Your Man

Suddenly the air fills with Tammy Wynette singing "Stand By Your Man." She drowns out the birds and the bees, oversings the tedium of traffic on the avenue. Most of us out and about sing along. After hours of this, packages in hand, I am ready to head home, taking the bus so I hold up at the stop where someone's reading the daily. It slowly lowers and the someone asks if I am the man. Yes, I guess I am, I reply. Stand here by me, he says, I am the man as well, your man, whether it's a partial remodel or from-the-ground-up new construction. Suddenly the air is quiet. Not a single bird or bee. Then pounding, pounding like you wouldn't believe.

Wind Being Wind

Heinrich had neither health nor wealth so instead of climbing a mountain in some faraway land, he took the stairs of the town's tallest building and walked to its top. What made it tough going were his walker getting caught on the stair treads and his knee brace constantly needing adjusting and, and he kept dropping things, his goggles and some protein bars and his Superman thermos filled with Tang but eventually Heinrich got to the top and laid a nice little flag on the chopper pad. Wind being wind awarded him its congratulatory burn. All the way down in the elevator he listened to what sounded like applause but was really the same wind rising up through the airshaft. Heinrich got a good write up in *The Herald* as well he should have since none of the town's founders had ever done this before, not for lack of trying.

How The Great Chefs of Pennsylvania Got Started

I told the reporter with the horn rims and the handheld I looked out the window over the sink while sipping my very first cup and there they were, maybe a hundred of them, potatoes, the big baking kind, plopped down all over the lawn and before I could get out there without spilling anything, pigs came traipsing in through the fence breaks and began gobbling them up and all I had on my porch steps were cabbages, ones picked a few days ago, and I began heaving them into this makeshift volleyball court the pigs had made of my outback and a shoat showed me and everyone watching what a hell of a spiker he was, despite his lesser girth and the neighbor across the alley called him his little fuzzy-wuzzy dumplin' which for some reason embarrassed even me and soon all the potatoes had been wolfed down and all the pigs had gone home to whatever pig county they had come from and with the reporter still filming, I plopped down on my porch steps, turning the remaining cabbages over and over in my hands, occasionally tossing one into the air, then two or three at the same time, then four.

Sea Dogs

Jonas met himself a siren out by the rocks, you know the ones I mean, the craggy ones with all the mussels. He learned soon enough not to ruffle her scales when they were going at it in the dory. Being the impulsive sea lover he is, he asked her to marry him and without hesitation she said aye. When not out there among the splashing waves, Jonas pushed her around in a wheelchair with a bell and little turn signals, having been inspired by the Divine Miss M one evening in Rehoboth. Jonas was often seen combing his siren's yard-long locks in which he sometimes got tangled and one time the untangling led to them doing it right there on the dock where both got arrested with their names in the weekly. She, it turned out, was really Janet from across the sound. Jonas was always Jonas from right here in town and he came to love Janet more every day, she being a real woman and all and of course Jonas having always been a real man.

Keeping It Holy

Sunday while his family goes to church, Keith slips off to Party City, the most wonderful fun store in the world and there's this Jesus look-alike who works there, Keith always sees him in the aisles arranging the merchandise, trying on a party wig and costume, setting up a sample table for twelve with paper and plastic and Jesus look-alike always offers Keith treats and he and Keith chew with their mouths open and talk about what makes them happy and at least once a visit, Jesus look-alike lets Keith rise up with him on his hydraulic lift to the high shelves ten or twelve feet off the floor and it's like being at the top of a rainbow's arch and when Keith leaves the store at the end of the hour, no one's been closer to heaven.

Dive or No Dive

Everyone suiting up has already eaten. Not me, I'll eat later after I touch down and true to my word, I tuck and roll onto the roof of Dale's Waffle House, much to the dismay of my team leader, not to mention six of Dale's steady customers looking out through the clerestory plus Dale himself so I pay for their breakfasts and tell them just what it's like jumping into thin air, seeing everything at your feet, but not your feet get bigger and bigger, and after eaters throw up a little on their toast-wiped clean plates, Dale takes me to the roof where together we fold my parachute into what becomes a swan, a most beautiful and elegant swan and the largest either of us has ever seen which we immediately spray down with starch to set up overnight to become the beacon for Dale's new Diving Swan Diner serving breakfast all hours and free to anyone just dropping in.

Business Major

At age ten and at eleven o'clock in the morning Archie set out in slightly damp clothes and spit-shined shoes to steal one of everything from the Five and Dime, yesteryear's Dollar General, until he had enough stuff to start his own little variety in an abandoned rusty bus in that hayfield, you know the one along Route 9, so come his twelfth birthday Archie celebrated his grand opening, mostly with the other punks on the block who robbed him silly but what most didn't know was Archie got the old rust bucket running again so he ran the punks down all along Route 4, really just maimed them a little because he needed their steals to restock, meanwhile picking their pockets while they were just coming to as nobody remembered what hit them so Archie made out that day, made out supremely when he sold out to the guidance counselor and acting vice principal.

Virtuosity

When Guy played his cello outdoors, its sound was as rich and deep as the soil the cello's endpin sunk into, different from when he played on a stage's plank floor, different yet from the harder sound when he played on the sidewalk downtown and simply otherworldly when he plucked and strummed it across his lap like a big bull guitar but when he stuck it like a violin under his chin, its endpin jabbed his carotid and he nearly bled out and had it not been for the man on the park bench who slapped his sandwich over the wound like a compress, Guy would not have switched to the harp, or was it the piano, he could never be sure, he knew it was something he couldn't pick up, no wait, it was the best-of-the-line air conditioner with its infinite settings stuck in the window looking out from his bedroom over the whole of downtown.

Me as Pearl

Sid gets lost each time he takes a walk. He's got this tail you see, well, he wears this oversized trench coat all the time whose lining's ripped and drags behind him and it rearranges things as he goes along so when he turns around to return, everything looks different. What about footprints, don't you leave any, I ask him, your big boot treads always clogged with mud? Nope, Sid says, the mud's all mine and I am going to keep it. So, how do you get home then? I ask, and Sid says, home is in the moment, he speaks like some old guru, home is where the heart it, home is sweet. So now we're found, I say, you and me together in this place and Sid says, sonny boy we're never lost, right now we're simply standing here in line in Long John Silver's that hasn't moved for hours waiting for some crusty scrod and hush puppies, don't forget those hushpuppies, you can pop out of my pocket now, the whole world's an oyster.

Momentary Bliss

Buddy Jack says he's getting off this merry-go-round called life and taking a ride on the rollercoaster I call death so I tell him I'll wait over there by that tree where I get all stretched out with a beer and a smoke in one hand and comic book in the other, don't call me unless there's blood, and so the afternoon plays on and neither of us sees hide nor hair of the other until it's almost dark when we meet back at the pickup under the vapor lamp but neither of us knows who the other is which leads to all sorts of complications like whose pickup is it, who's going to drive, hey, that's my hat, those, my binoculars, let's get the hell home as the wives, we do remember we have wives, will have supper on and the kids, we've sort of forgotten the kids, will have run away again, and again we'll be eating with the cops.

Wilds

I went for a walk yesterday when a flock of wild turkeys flew over my head and landed feet first on my path. Then a commotion of wild dogs chasing wild hogs gathered around my legs but moved past, now hogs chasing dogs fleeing one lone wild cat with a tail that spun like a propeller. Now all I could think of were the wild one-eyed Jacks I drew to win a poker pot last Friday night, that and a wild hair up my ass kept me steady on my path that I'd long ago chosen instead of calm, the mere contemplation of calm left me blank in search of breath. What good is breath if you cannot pant? Just then a wild goose flew over and dropped an egg in my cap. I held it up and yelled, thanks. Days later its shell cracked and a good looking little gosling sang in my arms. "Born to be wild" was all I made out. I sang back, "Wild thing, I think I love you," knowing the score.

Jungle in Here

Ernie's got this dive downtown where all us misfits go to have a few, make out a little, nothing heavy because if Ernie sees it getting heavy, he shows up at our backs and tells us, take it outside because inside, the only talk is touch starting with a tap on the shoulder, then a grin, one with teeth, as many as you got, a tilt of the head, heads, but no kisses because he only wants our lips licking lips of bottles, then there he is, swinging hand over hand across the exposed plumbing among the ceiling rafters he purposely never concealed, Ernie having been one of the ten TV Tarzans, hand over hand he goes over a pile of dogs, cat in heat, parrot, parakeet, drink your drinks, he shrieks, then get out but come back, don't forget to come back, you, you animals you.

Acknowledgments

Apalachee Review: "Lost Gnosis"
Blueline (SUNY Potsdam): "Great Whale"
Burningword Literary Journal: "Wilds"
Evening Street Review: "Garage Man," "Bobbing Dead"
Front Range Review: "Bugs in the Night"
The Lumberyard: "Paper Opera"
Moonstone Nonsense Verse Anthology 2021: "Local Physics"
Moonstone Ink Anthology 2021: "To the Shoes"
Quarter After Eight: "Big Game," "The Door"
RFD: "Sweet Potato," "Straight Shooting"
Rabid Oak: "Name on It," "Virtuosity," "No Need for Intros"
Rat's Ass Review: "Jungle in Here"
Salt River Review: "Rooming"
Spank the Carp: "Keeping It Holy"
Squawk Back: "Brads," "Empties," "Kissin Cous"
Stickman Review: "My Father as Car"
Stirring: A Literary Collection: "Fountain for Youth"
Streetlight: "Sunday Drive"
Third Wednesday: "All It Takes"
Triggerfish Critical Review: "Man in Blue"
Zillah: "Marks"

Title Index

First Line Index

A

B

C

D

E

F

H

I

S

T

V

W

Y

www.ingramcontent.com/pod-product-compliance
Lightning Source LLC
Chambersburg PA
CBHW010046090426
42735CB00020B/3400
* 9 7 8 1 5 9 4 9 8 1 4 1 8 *